THE BIRTHDAY LADY

by Ada Evelyn
illustrated by Cameron Eagle

Scott Foresman

Editorial Offices: Glenview, Illinois • New York, New York
Sales Offices: Reading, Massachusetts • Duluth, Georgia
Glenview, Illinois • Carrollton, Texas • Menlo Park, California

Hi, there! Here I am.

The Birthday Lady!

So that is Binky! I hear that today is his birthday. Yes, it is his special day. I hope he is ready.

Shh! Don't wake him up! We need to talk secretly anyway. Cats love to sleep. Binky is very good at it.

I know you just love him. Let's give Binky the best birthday ever!

You can help me get everything ready.

Balloons! Balloons! We need
lots of large balloons.

Ribbons! Ribbons! We need lots of them too.

Here is the special cake.
How do you like it?

I made it with large cans of cat food. This will get his attention. Binky will love it!

Here are the presents! Every birthday cat needs presents.

Come on, helper! You can open a
present for Binky! It will be interesting.

Now, don't yell surprise!
Cats have very good ears. They
like whispers best. Ready?

Happy Birthday!